IT'S TIME TO EAT CRAB RANGOON

It's Time to Eat
CRAB RANGOON

Walter the Educator

Silent King Books
A WhichHead Entertainment Imprint

Copyright © 2024 by Walter the Educator

All rights reserved. No part of this book may be reproduced in any manner whatsoever without written per- mission except in the case of brief quotations embodied in critical articles and reviews.

First Printing, 2024

Disclaimer

This book is a literary work; the story is not about specific persons, locations, situations, and/or circumstances unless mentioned in a historical context. Any resemblance to real persons, locations, situations, and/or circumstances is coincidental. This book is for entertainment and informational purposes only. The author and publisher offer this information without warranties expressed or implied. No matter the grounds, neither the author nor the publisher will be accountable for any losses, injuries, or other damages caused by the reader's use of this book. The use of this book acknowledges an understanding and acceptance of this disclaimer.

It's Time to Eat CRAB RANGOON is a collectible early learning book by Walter the Educator suitable for all ages belonging to Walter the Educator's Time to Eat Book Series. Collect more books at WaltertheEducator.com

USE THE EXTRA SPACE TO TAKE NOTES AND DOCUMENT YOUR MEMORIES

CRAB RANGOON

Crab Rangoon, all crispy and hot,

It's Time to Eat
Crab Rangoon

A golden treat that hits the spot.

Wrapped up tight, like a treasure inside,

With creamy filling that cannot hide.

Take a bite and feel the crunch,

Crab Rangoon is fun to munch!

Creamy crab with a hint of cheese,

A warm little snack, sure to please.

Inside the filling, soft and smooth,

Each bite is a tasty groove.

Wrapped in dough, fried to brown,

Crab Rangoon never lets us down!

Dip it in sauce, sweet or tangy,

Each little piece is simply dandy.

The wrapper's thin, the edges crisp,

A perfect snack with every twist.

It's Time to Eat
Crab
Rangoon

Crab Rangoon, shaped like a star,

A tasty treat from near or far.

Folded up tight with love and care,

A crunchy bite we love to share.

It's warm and golden, so much fun,

Crab Rangoon for everyone!

Inside there's crab, creamy and light,

Each little bite is pure delight.

Gather around, the platter's full,

Crab Rangoon is oh-so-cool.

With friends or family, it's the best,

Crab Rangoon beats all the rest!

A flavor so rich, a taste so fine,

Crab and cheese in every line.

Each crispy bite brings us cheer,

It's Time to Eat Crab Rangoon

Crab Rangoon time is finally here!

A little pillow, crunchy and sweet,

Filled with joy we're ready to eat.

Crab Rangoon's a yummy tune,

Perfect treat for afternoon!

So take a bite and feel the crunch,

Crab Rangoon is fun to munch.

A golden snack for me and you,

It's Time to Eat Crab Rangoon

Crab Rangoon, we love you too!

ABOUT THE CREATOR

Walter the Educator is one of the pseudonyms for Walter Anderson. Formally educated in Chemistry, Business, and Education, he is an educator, an author, a diverse entrepreneur, and he is the son of a disabled war veteran. "Walter the Educator" shares his time between educating and creating. He holds interests and owns several creative projects that entertain, enlighten, enhance, and educate, hoping to inspire and motivate you. Follow, find new works, and stay up to date with Walter the Educator™

at WaltertheEducator.com

www.ingramcontent.com/pod-product-compliance
Lightning Source LLC
LaVergne TN
LVHW052011060526
838201LV00059B/3974